GULLIBLE'S TRAVELS

A Preface Toward the Recovery of

Biblical Eschatology

By Rev. James DuJack

Printed in the United States of America

First Printing, 2012

ISBN-13: 978-0615673189
ISBN-10: 061567318X

Oakwood Covenant Press
260 Oakwood Avenue
Troy, NY 12182

Scripture Quotations are from The Holy Bible,

King James Version

The following is a re-working of a sermon delivered at Oakwood Bible Church on August 12th, 2001 by Rev. James DuJack

Dedication

Though I've preached for some twenty five years, this marks my first formal venture into the publishing world. Preaching and publishing are very separate endeavors, yet for me each has required the support of one supremely fitted as a wonderful helpmeet. This work therefore, is dedicated to Karen, my wife. She is my virtuous woman, whose value is far above rubies. She is all that Solomon wrote of, and more. Imagine what he would have written had he known that she also could type!

Contents:

Chapter 1   Gulliver

Chapter 2   Gullible

Chapter 3   The Church on Track

Chapter 4   The Church off Track

Chapter 5   Be Bereans

Chapter 1: Gulliver

"Beloved, believe not every spirit, but try the spirits whether they are of God; because many false prophets are gone out into the world. Hereby know ye the Spirit of God: Every spirit that confesseth that Jesus Christ is come in the flesh is of God. And every spirit that confesseth not that Jesus Christ is come in the flesh is not of God: and this is that spirit of antichrist, whereof ye have heard that it should come; and even now already is it in the world. Ye are of God, little children, and have overcome them: because greater is he that is in you, than he that is in the world." 1 John 4:1-4

Have you ever heard of Jonathan Swift? He was an Anglican Minister, born in 1667 who wrote the book Gulliver's Travels. As a minister he was at war with unbelief and all of the non-Christian elements that were then present in Great Britain.

Believing that the pen was mightier than the sword, he wrote both prolifically and prophetically. Most of his writing was political satire aimed at ridiculing in a humorous way the politicians, the ruling class, the professors, and the scientists of his day. His best known work is Gulliver's Travels, which revealed great connection and resemblances to the issues he faced in England.

There are actually four adventures to the work known as <u>Gulliver's Travels</u>. The first is the most well-known. Gulliver is shipwrecked and stranded on an island inhabited by people one twelfth his size, (about six inches tall). He is tied up with ropes by these tiny people. The other adventures it seems to me are less well known.

Adventure number two, which many are still familiar with, takes Gulliver to a place where he is one twelfth the size of others, (he is six inches tall). He becomes a pet doll for a princess.

In adventure number three, Gulliver finds three kingdoms. It is a very strange place, with very odd people. Some view this adventure as set in the Orient, perhaps in Japan.

Remember; England in the 1700's was isolated by today's standards. People truly wondered what and who might be on the other side of the world. Gulliver's adventures were even believed by many people, such was the ignorance, or should I say the gullibility of the people of his day.

Adventure number four, at least to my mind, reinforces the old adage, "the more things change the more they stay the same". In adventure number four, Gulliver discovers a land ruled by horses! Then there are also strange and savage animals they called yahoos. These yahoos bare close resemblance to human beings. As I thought about this, I said to myself: a land dominated and ruled by horses, strange and savage yahoos who look like people. I know, he's talking about Saratoga, NY, it's August and it's the place to be!

Chapter 2: Gullible

Why am I telling you all this? Gulliver's Travels took him to many strange, exotic, fascinating, and even fun places. There was only one problem, none of it was real. I want you to remember this because Christians, if they are not careful, can take Gullible's Travels and end up in similar, strange and fanciful places. Places that likewise are not real.

Two things marked his adventures. What can we say about the first two? These first two deal with the issue of **proportion**. Seeing things out of proportion. Things were twelve times bigger and then twelve times smaller. It may be fun, fascinating, strange, even exotic, but it is not real.

Gulliver's second two adventures are marked not so much by things out of proportion, but by things out of **place**. There were strange kingdoms and territories, and horses in leadership. These things as well may be fascinating, fun, and exotic but they are equally not real.

Christian, you are warned in this passage

not be gullible. Sadly, many Christians are on their own <u>Gullible's</u> <u>Travels</u>. All it takes is for information, even Biblical information, maybe from another spiritual person to send you on this adventure. **All it takes is a little information, a little bit out of proportion and a little bit out of place and your Christian experience can be a great adventure with none of it being real!**

I said, Christian you are warned in the above passage not to be gullible, and I address you as Christians, as God does, as St. John does in verse 1, (***Beloved***). What he says in love there, I say in love today. What else does he say? "*Beloved*, ***believe not***"; actually in the Greek it is stronger than that. It says: "*stop believing*". They already were being taken in, they already were too gullible. He says; "*stop believing*"!

Do you believe everything you are told? Do you believe every preacher? Do you believe every radio program? Should you?

Turn over to Galatians 1:6-9. "*I marvel that ye are so soon removed from him that called you into the grace of Christ unto another gospel. Which is not another; but there be some that trouble you, and would pervert the gospel of Christ. But though we, or an angel from heaven, preach any other gospel unto you than that which we have preached unto you, let him be accursed. As we said before, so say I now again, if any man preach any other gospel unto you than that ye have received, let him be accursed.*"

How about Acts 17:10 & 11. *"And the brethren immediately sent away Paul and Silas by night unto Berea: who coming thither went into the synagogue of the Jews. These were more noble than those in Thessalonica, in that they received the word with all readiness of mind, and searched the scriptures daily, whether those things were so."*

You know, our culture likes to praise and applaud people who are *"persons of faith"*. But faith in what? Charles Manson is a person of faith; he believes that he is Jesus Christ. Is that the kind of person of faith we ought to praise and applaud? You see to praise and applaud *"faith"*, blindly and generically is to be a great supporter of our cultural polytheism. Many gods, everything is a god, anything is a god.

Do you know that the early Christians were considered atheists? They honored none of the cultural and visible gods of their day! To be a Christian however, as opposed to merely being a person of faith, is to be like Christ, right? A Christian therefore is, are you ready? I am going to say it, I've got to say it, a Christian is a discriminator by definition and by commandment. Christ was a discriminator. He posited right and wrong. He also commands us to be discriminating!

If this sounds like hate speech to you, it's because you want the world to be something that it is not. Dealing with Biblical reality requires maturity. We are to be discerners. We are to be discriminators. We are to see the world in right proportion. We are to hold His truths in their right place. If we don't do this, we individually and/or corporately as churches, launch off on Gullible's Travels. We then spend all our time on detours instead of the work of dominion.

Chapter 3: The Church on Track

The Church of Jesus Christ, though stressed and swayed, has historically stayed on track. Let's examine what G.K. Chesterton wrote:

"The church in its early days went fierce and fast with any war horse; yet it is utterly unhistoric to say that she merely went mad along one idea, like a vulgar fanaticism. She swerved to left and right, so exactly as to avoid enormous obstacles. She left on one hand the huge bulk of Arianism, buttressed by all the worldly powers to make Christianity too worldly. The next instant she was swerving to avoid an orientalism, which would have made it too unworldly. The orthodox church never took the tame course or accepted the conventions; the orthodox church was never respectable. It would have been easier to have accepted the early power of the Arians. It would have been easy in the Calvinistic seventeenth century, to fall into the bottomless pit of predestination. It is easy to be a madman: it is easy to be a heretic. It is always easy to let the age have its head; the difficult thing is to keep one's own. It is always easy to be a modernist; as it is easy to be a snob. To have fallen into any of those open traps of error and exaggeration which fashion after fashion and sect after sect set along the historic path of Christendom – that would indeed have been simple. It is always simple to fall; there are an infinity of angels at which one falls, only one at which one stands. To have fallen into any one of the fads from Gnosticism to Christian Science would indeed have been obvious and tame. But to have

avoided them all has been one whirling adventure; and in my vision the heavenly chariot flies thundering through the ages, the dull heresies sprawling and prostrate, the wild truth reeling but erect."[1]

The Bible, not false prophets, provides what is real. The Church, not the world, provides true adventure. The Church has kept things in proportion and in place. St. John warns us, even as he warned those of his day about false prophets, even antichrists. Now, lest we put them in the wrong place, let's make sure we see that St. John places them in his time![2]

Verse 1: **false prophets are gone out.**
"Beloved, believe not every spirit, but try the spirits whether they are of God; because many false prophets are gone out into the world."

Verse 3: **even now, already is.** *"And every spirit that confesseth not that Jesus Christ is come in the flesh is not of God: and this is that spirit of antichrist, whereof ye have heard that it should come; and even now already is it in the world."*

---

[1] G.K. Chesterton's "Orthodoxy"

[2] Don't forget to note that in all of the Bible, St. John is the only author who references "antichrist", and that only in his tiny epistles! The Book of Revelation does not reference "antichrist" and, that work too is largely concerned with first century matters.

Chapter 4: The Church off Track

To place the antichrist exclusively in our future and to focus ceaselessly on that may be exciting, stimulating, fearful, motivating; but it isn't real because it is out of place. It may fill churches, it appeals to our egotism, narcissism, and hyper sense of self importance, that the journey ahead for us is an exceptional journey. It makes our generation the terminal generation. That however, would be a journey that only Gullible would go on.

I know, I was on that journey a generation ago and the Jupiter effect of 1982 did not cause the earth or its orbit to convulse! Too much "Biblical truth" was simply and sadly theories of men, which were all attempting to scare people into the kingdom.

Note Isaiah 29:13 *"Wherefore the Lord said, Forasmuch as this people draw near me with their mouth, and with their lips do honour me, but have removed their heart far from me, and their fear toward me is taught by the precept of men."[3]*

---

[3] I wish more expositors would pay as much attention to the closing words of this verse as they do the opening words.

Hear me clearly, I said those holding the antichrist as an exclusively future phenomena and focusing on that! I do not doubt the work of antichrist in spirits in the world today or Satan's final rebellion. I simply know that the Bible focuses on the **then** present work of antichrist. Not only on the **then** present work of the enemy, but also the **then** victorious work of the Christians over the enemy.

Look at verse four of 1 John 4:4 *"Ye are of God, little children, and have overcome them; because greater is he that is in you, than he that is in the world."*

Y*ou "have overcome them"*; this is not wishful thinking, but accomplished fact. Furthermore, the word overcome is special to St. John. It appears six times in this little book of 1 John, and it challenges each of the seven churches addressed in Revelation.[4] Every church, every Christian is to be an overcomer. The Greek word is related to our " NIKE", (think sneakers, hats and tee shirts). In Christ, Christians are victors, overcomers, conquerors, and those who prevail. All this points to victory over the world, the flesh and the devil, which includes the false prophets and the antichrist. To fearfully embrace and promote the rule of

---

[4] David Chilton's "Days of Vengeance" page 98-99, and throughout illustrates the even greater pervasiveness of Nikao.

antichrist is to be as gullible as believing that horses rule! It may fill churches and bookstores but something is greatly out of place.

Chapter 5: Be Bereans

We don't want to view things out of place. We also don't want to view them out of proportion. Remember Gulliver; first twelve times bigger and then twelve times smaller. Satan is an enemy. Satan is alive. After what I've been through, I know that Satan is more powerful than we in ourselves as mere humans, but Satan is no match for the Spirit of God! We must keep this in proportion. He's not nothing, as some purport. He's not almighty, as others might have you to think.

What a great statement of relation and proportion the Bible gives us! In verse four: "*because greater*", (thank God); the word "greater" describes relation; proportion. "Greater is He that is in you than He that is in the world".

Beloved Brethren: the early 1700's were a time of great invention, adventure, and exploration. So are the early 2000's. Brethren, let us be Bereans.

Acts 17:10 & 11 *"And the brethren immediately sent away Paul and Silas by night unto Berea: who coming thither went into the synagogue of the Jews. These were more noble than those in Thessalonica, in that, they received the word with all readiness of mind, and searched the scriptures daily, whether those things were so".*

Let us not be ignorant. Let us not be gullible. We have been told to occupy and that He will take care of the rest. The real travels, the real adventure that God would have us be on is so much better than the pretend. Don't worry about being left behind from a pretend journey!

We are called to be believers! You know, some in the 1700's believed too much and some in the 2000's believe too much. Beloved brethren, **"believe not"**, **"stop believing"** every spirit, but test them, try them, see if they be of God.